History's Mysteries

THE DINOSAUR EXTINCTION
WHAT REALLY HAPPENED?

MEGAN COOLEY PETERSON

BLACK RABBIT BOOKS

Bolt is published by Black Rabbit Books
P.O. Box 3263, Mankato, Minnesota, 56002.
www.blackrabbitbooks.com
Copyright © 2019 Black Rabbit Books

Jennifer Besel, editor; Grant Gould, designer;
Omay Ayres, photo researcher

Library of Congress Cataloging-in-Publication Data
Names: Peterson, Megan Cooley, author.
Title: The dinosaur extinction : what really happened? / by Megan Cooley
Peterson. Description: Mankato, Minnesota : Black Rabbit Books, [2019]
| Series: Bolt. History's mysteries | "Bolt is published by Black Rabbit
Books." | Audience: Age 8-12. | Audience: Grade 4 to 6. | Includes
bibliographical references and index. | Description based on print version
record and CIP data provided by publisher; resource not viewed.
Identifiers: LCCN 2017036492 (print) | LCCN 2017042719 (ebook) |
ISBN 9781680725247 (ebook) | ISBN 9781680724080 (library binding) |
ISBN 9781680727029 (paperback)
Subjects: LCSH: Dinosaurs—Extinction—Juvenile literature. |
Dinosaurs—Juvenile literature. Classification: LCC QE861.6.E95 (ebook) |
LCC QE861.6.E95 P48 2019 (print) | DDC 567.9—dc23
LC record available at https://lccn.loc.gov/2017036492

Printed in China. 3/18

Image Credits
Alamy: Science Photo Library, 12;
Science Picture Co, 24–25 (dino); Stocktrek
Images, 4–5, 21; bbcearth.com: 15; Dreamstime:
Corey A. Ford, 22; Masato Hattori: 18–19; Science
Source: Francois Gohier, 9 (t); Shutterstock: Airin.dizain,
10–11 (bkgd); Aksenova Natalya, 24 (l); Alex Leo, Cover
(stars); Antracit, 3; AuntSpray, 26; Catmando, 10–11 (silhou-
ettes); dkvektor, 10–11 (bkgd); Herschel Hoffmeyer, Cover
(dino), 16–17 (t); Maria Isaeva, Cover, 29 (magnifying glass);
Natsmith1, 29 (dino); Oleg Golovnev, 29 (paper); Photomontage,
6–7; Quick Shot, 24–25 (bkgd); Sakhno Vadim, 9 (bm); Sofia
Santos, 31; Suradech Prapairat, 9 (bl); Ton Bangkeaw, 1, 32; Twin
Design, 9 (br); VectorShow, 16–17 (b); wallpaperscraft.com:
Soko Y Brother, 6 (t)
Every effort has been made to contact copyright holders
for material reproduced in this book. Any omissions
will be rectified in subsequent printings if
notice is given to the
publisher.

CONTENTS

CHAPTER 1

DISAPPEARING
Dinosaurs

Dinosaurs once ruled Earth. Some were huge. Others were only the size of turkeys. Then, about 65 million years ago, every dinosaur disappeared. What happened to these **ancient reptiles**?

People in ancient China found dinosaur fossils. But they didn't know about dinosaurs then. They thought the fossils belonged to dragons.

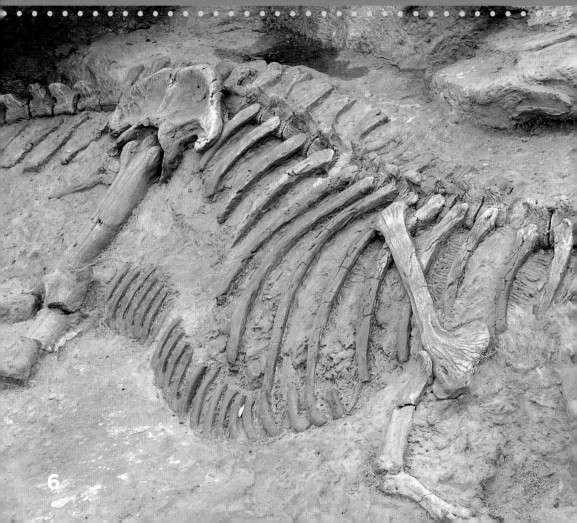

6

A Mystery

People know dinosaurs existed because of fossils. Dinosaur fossils have been found on every continent. By studying them, scientists know dinosaurs lived between 230 and 65 million years ago. But they don't know what killed these creatures.

CHAPTER 2

FINDING Fossils

Scientists study fossils to learn how dinos lived. One dig site contained about 10,000 Hadrosaur skeletons. These duck-billed dinosaurs lived in groups.

Fossils show that dinosaurs laid eggs. Adults might have cared for some young dinos. Others lived and grew on their own.

Comparing Egg Sizes···►

2 inches
(5 centimeters)
long

6 inches
(15 cm)
long

12 inches
(30 cm)
long

average
chicken egg

average
ostrich egg

largest dino
egg found

DINOSAUR DISCOVERIES

Paleontologists have found dinosaur fossils around the world. Here are some of the top sites.

JURASSIC COAST
in Great Britain

MORRISON FORMATION
in the United States

VALLE DE LA LUNA
in Argentina

DASHANPU FORMATION
in China

TENDAGURU FORMATION
in Tanzania

DINOSAUR COVE
in Australia

CHAPTER 3

INVESTIGATING the Cause

Dinosaurs vanished about 65 million years ago. But what happened? One idea is that a large **asteroid** struck Earth. Scientists found a large **crater** in Mexico. The crater is about 125 miles (201 kilometers) wide!

Too Cold

An asteroid crash would have thrown soil and dust into the air. The dust blocked the sun's rays. Earth cooled, and plants couldn't grow. The dinosaurs may have run out of food.

Scientists have found iridium near fossils. This metal is common in asteroids.

Dinosaurs have nowhere to go.

Lava flows destroy land.

16

Erupting Volcanoes

Some scientists blame volcanoes. Volcanoes spit out lava and gases. Huge lava flows might have covered many miles of land. Gases, ash, and dust may have blocked the sun and cooled Earth. The dinosaurs could not survive the cold climate.

Gas and ash block sun's rays.

WHEN DINOSAURS LIVED

MESOZOIC ERA

Triassic Period (251-199 million years ago)		Jurassic Period (199-145 million years ago)	
Coelophysis Plateosaurus		Allosaurus Brachiosaurus Stegosaurus	

| MILLIONS OF YEARS AGO | 251 | 199 | 145 |

Cretaceous Period

(145-65 million years ago)

Triceratops

Tyrannosaurus Rex

Velociraptor

145

65

PRESENT

Taking a Long Time to Hatch

Eggs may have also led to the dinosaurs' downfall. Researchers guess some dino eggs took six months to hatch. Eggs were easy meals for **predators**. Eggs also couldn't survive harsh weather. Without new young, dino populations would have fallen.

A Changing Landscape

Shifting continents may have also killed the dinosaurs. During the Cretaceous period, oceans pulled away from land. Sea levels dropped. Earth probably became cooler and drier. Maybe dinosaurs couldn't **adapt** to a cooler planet.

Not Really Gone?

Not everyone believes all the dinosaurs died out. Some people think dinosaurs **evolved**. Modern-day birds might have come from dinosaurs called **theropods**. Tyrannosaurus rex was a giant theropod.

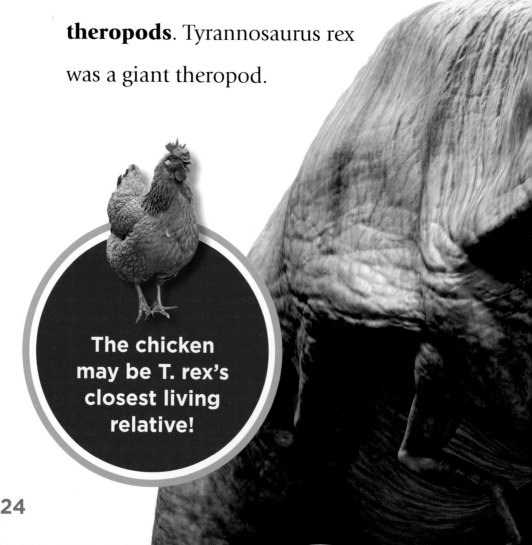

The chicken may be T. rex's closest living relative!

Other animals, like mammals and small reptiles, lived alongside dinosaurs. Why didn't they die out? That's another history mystery!

CHAPTER 4

You DECIDE

Scientists have many ideas about what killed the dinosaurs. Did a huge asteroid hit Earth? Did volcanoes spew gases and lava? Researchers continue to look for clues. Maybe one day, people will know the answers to this mystery.

Asking Questions to Solve the Mystery

Researchers ask questions to solve history's mysteries. You can too!

 Who is studying fossils today?

 What do fossils tell us about dinosaurs?

 When did dinosaurs go extinct?

 Where did dinosaurs live?

WHY?

Why did dinosaurs die out?

HOW?

How did dinosaurs live?

What other questions do you have?

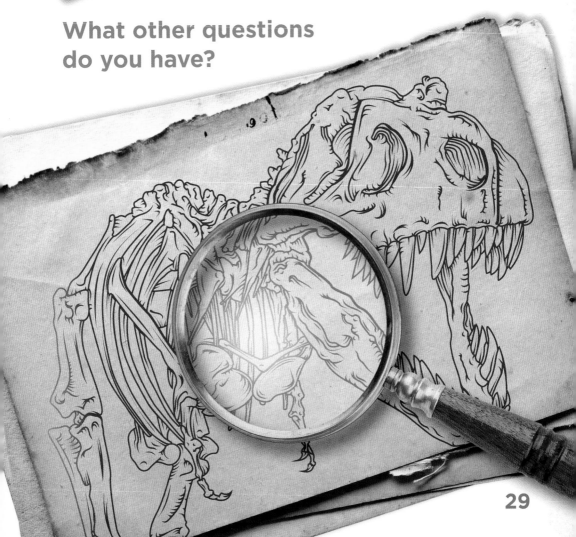

GLOSSARY

adapt (uh-DAPT)—to change something so it works better or is better suited for a purpose

ancient (AYN-shunt)—from a long time ago

asteroid (AS-tuh-royd)—a large space rock that moves around the sun

crater (KRAY-tuhr)—a large hole in the ground caused by something falling or exploding

evolve (ih-VOLV)—to slowly change

fossil (FAH-sul)—the remains or traces of plants and animals that are preserved as rock

paleontologist (pay-lee-ohn-TALL-uh-jist)—a scientist who studies fossils

predator (PRED-uh-tuhr)—an animal that eats other animals

reptile (REP-tile)—a cold-blooded animal that breathes air and has a backbone; most reptiles lay eggs and have scaly skin.

theropod (THERE-uh-pod)—a group of dinosaurs; theropods walked on two legs and ate meat.

BOOKS

Agresta, Jen, and Avery Elizabeth Hurt. *Dino Records: The Most Amazing Prehistoric Creatures Ever to Have Lived on Earth!.* National Geographic Kids. Washington, D.C.: National Geographic, 2017.

Peterson, Megan Cooley. *Dinosaurs.* Rank It! Mankato, MN: Black Rabbit Books, 2017.

Shofner, Melissa Raé. *Gareth's Guide to Unearthing a Dinosaur.* Gareth Guides to an Extraordinary Life. New York: Gareth Stevens Publishing, 2018.

WEBSITES

Dinosaurs
discoverykids.com/category/dinosaurs/

Dinosaurs and Prehistoric
kids.nationalgeographic.com/animals/hubs/dinosaurs-and-prehistoric/

Paleontology: The Big Dig
www.amnh.org/explore/ology/paleontology

INDEX